The Men Beyond the Stones

Stonehenge: Klickitat's WWI Memorial

The Men Beyond the Stones

Stonehenge: Klickitat's WWI Memorial

By

Andretta Schellinger

Copyright © 2019 by Andretta Schellinger

All rights reserved. No part of this publication may be reproduced, distributed, or transmitted in any form or by any means, including photocopying, recording, or other electronic or mechanical methods, without the prior written permission of the publisher, except in the case of brief quotations embodied in critical reviews and certain other noncommercial uses permitted by copyright law.

To contact author please email schellingerresearch@gmail.com

Published in the United States of America

ISBN: 9781795380331

Contents

Preface	i
Introduction	1
Evolution of World War I	3
Battles	7
Samuel Hill	9
James H. Allyn	15
Charles R. Auer	19
Dewey V. Bromley	25
John W. Cheshier	29
Richard E. Childs	32
William O. Clary	35
James D. Duncan	38
Harry Gotfredson	41
Robert F. Graham	46
Thomas E. Hovey	48
Louis Leidl	50
Carl A. Lester	55
Edward J. Lindblad	57
Henry O. Piendl	60
Robert F. Venable	65
Conclusion	67
Selected Bibliography	68
Appendix	70
About the Author	74

Preface

I decided to write this book because the first time I traveled to the Stonehenge replica near Maryhill, Washington, I wanted to know more. I wanted to know who these men were, why they are immortalized on stone, and what their stories are. My interest is in part due to being a historian, in part because I never stop thinking, and in part because I have a sociology degree and so I am always interested in the human aspect. Owning my own research company allows me to do genealogy research for friends and others whose histories intrigue me. We owe it to our communities to keep histories of our ancestors, be it family members, or strangers whose names are bronzed on cement structures overlooking the beautiful Columbia River.

This book was book in 2015 and then pushed to the side because of other books, events, and a full-time job teaching. No book is a solo effort, as a community of supporters and loved ones come together who wished to see me succeed in sharing these stories. I am fortunate enough to have a family who helps me when I need help and relaxes with me when the work gets to be too much. Without them, I do not think I would have written any of the books that I have, nor would I be in the position I am in today. Sometimes, other individuals with whom I was not well-acquainted came through when I needed them the most.

I had been working on genealogy for years, and I personally have traced my own family back to the 1700s. When I started working on research for this book, I realized that there wasn't a lot out there about these men or their families. I am now a contributing member of WikiTree, a free worldwide genealogy website whose goal is to connect each individual to a world tree that everyone is related to. For more information about these men's genealogy, search for them on WikiTree, where I have been personally adding all the ancestral information I can find. I started doing this in mid-2017 to mark research that I had done, and I found that I really enjoyed it.

Obviously my husband is to thank for helping with the structure of the individual chapters as well as moral support to keep going during moments of doubt. I also want to thank the National Personnel Records Center (NPRC) in St. Louis, Missouri, the repository for the majority of military records, including medical and official military records. Even though they were devastated by a fire that took place in 1973 that destroyed thousands of records, they assisted in getting the records needed for this in-depth look at these men's lives. Honestly, I also want to thank my daughter for her push with this project, because even if she doesn't help with chores all the time, and sometimes we wonder if she will reach her next birthday, she is amazing, and I wouldn't trade her for the world.

I debated whether to list the men's names in this book alphabetically or by the date they died. For ease of reading, I decided that alphabetical would be the best format because this book may be used as a resource, and that order keeps it simple. This is, of course, with an exception for Samuel Hill, who is the visionary and architect of Maryhill's Stonehenge. I felt that his profile being first would set the stage for the rest of the stories about the men who are included on the monument standing today.

During my research into World War I for my first book, I stumbled on a book of poetry written during the war by soldiers in the trenches. The book "A Muse in Arms," edited by E. B. Osborn, contains poetry mostly written by English service members, and the topics span ground, air, life, and death. While I included a few poems from this book in my aircraft book, an entirely different poem spoke to me for this book. Titled "The Home-coming," it speaks of the emotions that one takes from the battlefield when stepping foot on home soil. For those service members in this book whose lives were cut short in battle, they still returned at the hands of those who came out alive.

The Home-coming

When this blast is over-blown,

And the beacon fires shall burn

And in the street

Is the sound of feet–

They also shall return.

When the bells shall rock and ring,

When the flags shall flutter free,

And the choirs shall sing,

"God save our King"–

They shall be there to see.

When the brazen bands shall play,

And the silver trumpets blow,

And the soldiers come

To the tuck of the drum-

They shall be there also.

When that which was lost is found;

When each shall have claimed his kin,

Fear not they shall miss

Mother's clasp, maiden's kiss-

For no strange soil might hold them in.

When Te Deums seek the skies,

When the Organ shakes the Dome,

A dead man shall stand

At each live man's hand-

For they also have come home.

Joseph Lee

The Muse In Arms

1917

Introduction

Overlooking the Columbia River on the Washington border near Biggs, Oregon, there is a stone structure that resembles Stonehenge in Wiltshire, England. The truth is that it not only resembles it, but is a completed reproduction of the original Stonehenge.

Sam Hill, the eccentric creator of Maryhill Vineyards and Stonehenge, created this structure to replicate what Stonehenge may look like if it was completed. It was not just an homage to England, but also to a group of fourteen men whose names are permanently bronzed on the columns encircling the inner circle. One may think that these are individuals that Mr. Hill knew, but in actuality, Mr. Hill likely did not know them at all. All of these men have at least three things in common. One, they all heeded the call to arms for their nation during World War I. Two, these men had a connection to Klickitat County in South Central Washington. And three, they all lost their lives while in the service of the United States military. This replica by Mr. Hill was created to permanently immortalize these men, who came from different locations, backgrounds, and branches, and who all experienced different final moments.

This book is not about Sam Hill, although there is a chapter about him because he was the individual who created the Klickitat County Stonehenge. This book is about those who never came home, the real men behind the stones. It's not only about the fourteen men, but about their service, their youth, their families, and ultimately their untimely deaths.

During the research of the book, I discovered a lot of things that may surprise the reader, and some may not. It is unknown exactly how Sam Hill came about the names of the individuals, or if he knew the circumstances of their deaths. As you will find out, not all of our soldiers traveled to France. In fact, some died before even leaving Washington. Some of these men have still not returned home. Their remains are in France, either in a graveyard designated by Graves Registration Service (GRS), or they are still missing as one of the thousands of servicemen who, due to location and the confusion of war, are buried where they died.

Evolution of World War I

From chemical warfare to airplanes, the world saw new methods of destruction and medical advancements during World War I. To not take away from the individual stories of the service members, this chapter consists of details about the new aspects of the war that impacted at least one, if not several, of the men profiled in this book.

Identification Tags

World War I was the first war in which identification tags were issued to American service members. War Department Order No. 204 stated that any time a service member was wearing their field kit they were to wear at least one tag, which contained name, rank, and unit. The Army further added to this requirement with new regulations on July 6, 1916, that stated each service member was to have two identification tags, one to remain with the body and one to stay with the unit responsible for recordkeeping of all burials. During this time, identification tags could contain additional information, such as Charles Auer's, whose identification tag was stamped with what day he enlisted in the Marine Corps.

Burial Practices

During this war, when a service member was killed in action, it was initially the responsibility of their unit to bury the remains as soon as possible. This usually consisted of a shallow grave with the service member being buried in what he was wearing. Some units kept the identification tags with the remains, while others removed the tags in order to keep record of who was buried.

The US Army, in coordination with French Military Officials, began to further consolidate remains following November 11, 1918. This was done by disinterring remains from isolated graves and smaller plots and reinterring them in medium-sized cemeteries created by GRS along with the French Government. In total, eight cemeteries were created by GRS. Those eight still exist to this day.

Between 1919 and 1921, the United States sent letters to families of fallen service members, giving the option of having the remains returned to the United States. If elected, the remains could be interred in Arlington National Cemetery or returned to armed forces cemeteries located in the states, or to local cemeteries, usually with existing family plots.

For those with no family, or those whose families did not designate a wish for the remains to be returned, on March 4, 1923, President Harding signed legislation that created the American Battle Monuments Commission (ABMC), which was put in charge of creating monuments that honored the American Expeditionary Forces who gave their lives in Europe. While the cemeteries already existed, they were under the direction of the War Department, which changed hands with the creation of the ABMC. The ABMC not only took over daily care of the large memorials, but erected eleven monuments and two markers that commemorated significant battles and engagements.

Kelly Air Field

Before the United States joined in World War I, Kelly Field was nonexistent other than a small cotton field in San Antonio, Texas, that was only big enough for four small planes. From April 5 to May 7, 1917, the field consisted of tents and other temporary structures, with a slightly larger runway. On May 7, 400 men arrived to begin construction, but at that point, the United States had entered the war, and it was imperative that the Army had a place for its newly created aviation corps to train. By May 14, there were over 4,000 men on-site, with ground being cleared for larger buildings and more runways.

By late 1917 and into early 1918, Kelly Air Field became a proper airfield, with more than 325,000 servicemen in-processing, testing, and being organized into squadrons. Kelly Field was the premier place for pilots and flight instructors to learn the ropes, with 1,459 pilots and 398 flight instructors graduating within two short years.

Gold Star Family Pilgrimage

Beginning in World War I, a tradition began where the family of a service member would hang a flag with a blue star for each deployed family member. If one were to die during the war, the blue star would be changed to a gold one.

Widows and mothers of the fallen began to unofficially meet and call themselves the "Gold Star Mothers and Widows." These women began to create national organizations to help support those in need and to assist women in mourning for their loved ones. Following a successful campaign in Washington, D.C., Congress on March 2, 1929, authorized funds to allow wives and mothers, collectively known as "Gold Star Families," to visit the memorials created for the fallen.

Although all mothers and widows (who had not remarried) received an invitation, not all could travel. Between 1930 through 1933, the United States would pay for 6,654 women to travel to Europe where they visited **ABMC** monuments and cemeteries. Due to laws at the time, African American women were forced to travel separately from their white counterparts. Although there were protests from many Gold Star families, it did not stop 168 African American women from traveling.

Battles

While World War I was characterized by trench warfare, battles still waged that included only slight trench movement. For the purposes of this book, only battles in which the service members from Klickitat County fought in are included. Specific unit details are included with the profile of the service member who was actively part of a battle.

Bois de Belleau

The Battle of Bois de Belleau took place near the Marne River in France and consisted of two army divisions, including one brigade of US Marines. There were also elements from both the French 6th Army and the British IX Corps. The battle raged from June 1 to June 26, 1918, and resulted in 1,811 US service members killed and 7,966 wounded. An unknown number of German soldiers were killed or wounded, but the allied forces were able to capture 1,600. The battle was so fierce, and because of the tenacity of the United States Marines, France renamed the forest Bois de la Brigade de Marine, which is translated to Wood of the Marine Brigade. It was one of the first battles that really solidified the Marines as being the "deadliest weapon in the world" and as "remarkable marksmen" from not only American Expeditionary Forces (AEF) commanders, but also the German military.

Meurcy Farm

Following months of being in the trenches, General Pershing wanted to break the stalemate by going on the attack. Known as the Rainbow Division, the 42nd division first was in Chateau-Thierry while resting before receiving commands by Allied commander Ferdinand Foch who believed that the Germans were using Meurcy Farm as a staging area. They were ordered to drive forward beginning July 25, 1918, in hopes of pushing the Germans farther away from Paris. For five days, various regiments engaged in combat with the Germans who had fortified Meurcy Farm.

On July 28, believing that the Germans were in full retreat, the 165th infantry set to take a bank, only to find out the Germans had not left, and machine gun fire rained down on them. Even with high casualties, the 165th established the first foothold on the Eastern Bank, allowing the four other regiments to establish defensible positions. It was all for naught, for on July 29th, the Germans fought back, sending the 165th back over the river. It wasn't until July 30th that the 165th, along with the rest of the 42nd, were able to capture Meurcy Farm and with that, the region. In total, the battle took the lives of 184 officers and 5,469 men.

Samuel Hill

    Samuel Branson Hill is known for his involvement in Maryhill, a local establishment in Klickitat County, Washington, but there is much more to this man than meets the eye. In fact, many consider him as a manic individual who put everything into something, regardless of how it affected his personal life.

    Samuel Hill was born to Nathan Branson and Eliza Lenora (Mendenhall) Hill, a Quaker family in Deep River, North Carolina, on May 12, 1857. During the Civil War, his family was displaced, and they moved to Minneapolis, Minnesota, where he grew up. In 1878, Hill graduated from his father's alma mater, Haverford College, where he studied multiple languages as well as formal academic subjects such as mathematics, science, English, political science, and even rhetoric.

After graduating from Haverford College, he attended Harvard University for a year and earned a second bachelor's degree in 1879. After graduating, he returned home as a lawyer and took many jobs against the Great Northern Railway. After losing several lawsuits, the general manager of the company, James Hill, took a notice to Samuel and asked him to leave his current position and work as the railway's lawyer. While serving as the railway's lawyer, Samuel met and married James' daughter Mary in 1888.

For the next ten years, life was relatively mundane for Samuel. He and Mary had two children, Mary Mendenhall Hill in 1889 and James Nathan Branson Hill in 1893. Samuel assisted in many of his father-in-law's business endeavors, both at Great Northern Railway and at Minneapolis Trust Company, gaining wealth and connections that would serve him the rest of his life. In 1900, things seemed to fall apart between Samuel and his employer, James, and while they maintained a somewhat friendly business relationship, socially things began to take a turn downhill. Samuel determined that he would start traveling the world, and he traveled extensively in Europe and Canada. After visiting Russia, he decided he would settle down in Seattle. His wife did not want to, so she took their children back with her to the Midwest.

Hill gained his wealth buying and selling stock and businesses not only in Minneapolis, but also around the world. While most of them showed a return on investment, his purchase of a small region along the Columbia River never saw a return anywhere close to his investment. In 1907, Samuel bought up a small region in Klickitat County named Columbia, along the Columbia River. He named it

Maryhill, after his daughter and wife, although neither of them ever lived there, and may not have even visited.

Starting in the 1910s, Hill, while still maintaining his business ventures, began to advocate for paved roads in Washington State and Southern Canada. He also believed that the labor for paved roads should be completed by convicts to minimize costs. To assist with his advocacy, he used his property at Maryhill to show how effective paved roads can be. While many felt that this was a foolhardy move, this risk actually proved effective when he was able to persuade the University of Washington to create the nation's first chair for highway engineering. The state government in Washington, however, did not feel it was necessary to actually pave any roadways. The Oregon governor, Oswald Walt, was fascinated with what Hill was able to accomplish and began the construction of what is now known as the Historic Columbia River Highway (Hwy 30), which runs in Oregon from Astoria to The Dalles. Many parts of this highway system are still being utilized.

In 1914, on the anniversary of the Treaty of Ghent, Hill took it upon himself to embark on an international fundraising campaign among those he met during his travels, to assist in building the Peace Arch. With the funds raised, volunteers in 1920 began the construction of the Peace Arch with Hill dedicating the completed structure in 1921. This arch sits exactly on the Canadian and United States border between what is now Interstate 5 and Highway 99.

When residing in Minneapolis, Hill served as the Vice President for the Minneapolis Athenaeum, which at the time was a subscription-only, private library. By his position, he recruited George Putnam, the future librarian for the Library of Congress, to head up the Athenaeum. Over the course of his travels, Hill bought and then donated collections to the Athenaeum. Eventually, he purchased the stock from other owners and then donated it in its entirety to the public Minneapolis Foundation. The building has since been renamed the Minneapolis Central Library, one of the largest public libraries in the United States.

During his travels, Hill visited the English Stonehenge in 1915 with Britain's Secretary of State for War, Lord Horatio Herbert Kitchener. At the time, he believed that it was originally created as a sacrificial site. As a believer in the Quaker faith, he commissioned the monument in Klickitat County as a reminder that the God of War was still receiving the sacrifices of humanity. His desire was to not only represent humanity's sacrifice, but to also honor those who died during World War I, specifically those from Klickitat County, which Maryhill was part of. Prior to the dedication, Hill requested the presence of Professor W. Wallace Campbell from the Lick Observatory to determine the exact positioning of the altar stone so that it and all of the stones would be in perfect alignment for the summer solstice. The memorial was dedicated on July 4, 1918, and *The Goldendale Sentinel* ran the following article detailing the event:

> "To Klickitat County, Washington attaches the distinction of being the first community in the Northwest and so far as reported the first in America, to consecrate a memorial to its sons who have met death while in the nation's service in the existing war ... six names have already been inscribed upon the monument: Dewey V.

Bromley, John W. Cheshier, James B. Duncan, Robert F. Graham, Carl A. Lester, and Robert F. Venable. Space has been left for others who are expected in the nature of things to follow. Of these, 'One sleeps in the land where rolls the Oregon,' said Nelson B. Brooks, who made the chief dedicatory address, 'three in the soil of the pioneered hills of Klickitat, one upon the blood-stained hills of France, and one who, when the ocean gave up its dead from the torpedoed Tuscania, found a brutal place beneath the heather of Scotland.'"

The structure was built in the center of the town of Maryhill. Later, the town burned down, with only the concrete structure remaining. When the altar stone was inscribed, it was to honor the thirteen men directly and permanently. It reads, "To the memory of the soldiers and sailors of Klickitat County who gave their lives in the defense of their country...in hope that others inspired by the example of their valor and their heroism may share in that love of liberty and burn with that fire of patriotism which death alone can quench."

Samuel Hill (center) dedicating the altar stone and plaque.

While initially the stones only included six names, according to a newspaper article on Stonehenge at the time, seven more names were added on November 11, 1918. The thirteen remained that way until years later when the final individual, who fell in 1919, was immortalized. It was not until 1929 that the structure was complete, and a rededication ceremony took place on Memorial Day of that year.

Hill had initially believed that his Maryhill property would become a Quaker community, but with him being the only Quaker in the region, he likely soon realized that this was not a possibility. Hill began to build a mansion on the property, but he was stymied by both financial issues and the state of Washington's lack of highway development. One of his friends urged him to reconsider and he repurposed the building into an art museum. In 1926, Queen Marie of

Romania dedicated it, but it did not open until 1940, years after his death.

Stonehenge was not just a memorial for the fourteen men, but also for Hill. Upon his death in 1931, his remains were cremated and placed in a crypt below Stonehenge. Twenty-five years later, a new monument was placed on the location that reads "Samuel Hill: Amid nature's great unrest, he sought rest."

James H. Allyn

James Henry Allyn was born April 12, 1897, the third of Rufus and Sarah (Bogart) Allyn's five children.[1] He attended Goldendale Elementary, and greatly enjoyed the marching band. One thing that was consistent throughout his high school career was that he enjoyed playing a musical instrument.

On December 5, 1917, James walked into the Portland recruiter's office and enlisted in the Signal Corps, Aviation Section. That same afternoon, he was transported by bus to Vancouver Barracks

---

[1] James Allyn was not the first in his family to heed the call. Presumably, an uncle, James H. Allyn, enlisted during the Indian Wars. He served on the Pr. W. L. Buckley's 9 Oregon Mtd. Vol. He died during combat, and his widow, Mary, who also resided in Goldendale, was the recipient of a monthly stipend starting in 1902. In 1904, she moved to Bellingham, Washington, at the same time that her stipend increased to $12 a month.

to start the process of becoming a soldier. Following a week in Vancouver, which consisted of waiting for enough soldiers for the designated aviation section to justify a transport, Cpl. Allyn was bused along with other soldiers to Kelly Field in San Antonio, Texas. It took four days to travel from Washington to Texas. Although he was stationed in Texas, his official records showed that from December 6, 1917, to February 23, 1918, he was still attached to 5th Company (Co.), 2nd Motor Mechanics (MM) Regiment, A.S.S.C.

According to records, on February 24, 1918, Allyn was reassigned to 19th Co. 2nd MM Regiment, Signal Corps (SC) out of Camp Hancock, Georgia. It was during this time that he wrote letters home. On March 7, 1918, *The Goldendale Sentinel* published two letters to the editor. One from James Allyn himself, and one from his older brother, E. Valdie Allyn. James was writing to the editor in response to receiving the newspaper a short time before. In his letter, he detailed what had occurred since enlisting in Portland. Copies of those articles can be found in this book's appendix.

James Allyn was stationed in Georgia until March 13, 1918, when his unit was shipped out of Hoboken, New Jersey, on the USS Matsonia destined for France. Once in France, Cpl. Allyn was reassigned to the 5th Co. 2nd MM, SC, which he was part of until his death.

In France, he quickly contracted diphtheria and passed away in a French quarantine facility on July 15, 1918. The Army considered his death as being in the line of duty and not the result of his own misconduct, which meant that his family was able to collect death benefits. He was initially interred in Cemetery 159 near Romorantin, Grave A-3. Cpl. Allyn was buried with identification, and his grave was marked with a headboard with his name and service number on it.

Although his remains had not yet been returned, his family, having moved to Vancouver shortly prior to his death, returned to Goldendale to hold a memorial service in his name. His brothers, Valdie and Chester, were also in the military, the former being in the regular army stationed in San Diego and the latter as a volunteer stationed in France during his brother's death.

On October 1, 1920, the Pocahontas sailed from St. Nazaire with the remains of hundreds of American service members who lost their lives in France. Destined for Hoboken, New Jersey, the ship arrived on October 18, 1920, with the remains of James H. Allyn. On November 5, 1920, Cpl. Allyn's remains were transported along with eight others from Hoboken to Portland, Oregon. Following their arrival into Portland, Cpl. Allyn was then transported to Goldendale, Washington, where he arrived on November 14, 1920.

On September 10, 1937, James' brother Valdie, living in Olympia, applied for an upright headstone to be placed at the Odd Fellows Cemetery. The application was approved and the headstone was shipped on February 18, 1938, to Joseph H. Allyn living in Goldendale.

There had been a discrepancy on James Allyn's rank. Some of the documentation listed him as a private, while others had him as a corporal. For his final gravestone, Valdie requested confirmation regarding his rank. On November 23, 1937, the War Department determined that Cpl. James Allyn had been field promoted on May 1, 1918, and therefore he was a corporal when he died.

Cpl. James Allyn is permanently interred at the IOOF Mountain View Cemetery in Goldendale, Washington.

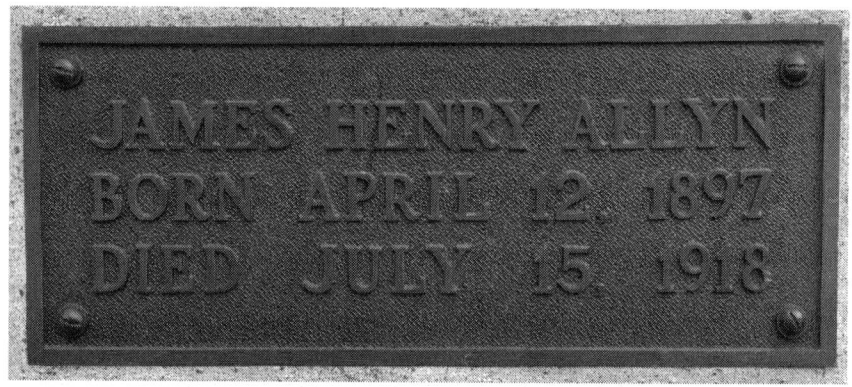

Charles R. Auer

Charles Auer was born to John F. and Mary Rosa (Newbill) Auer of Willamina, Oregon, on July 17, 1893.[2][3] He was the youngest of the couple's four children. In 1910, John moved his family to Hartland, a small town in Klickitat County, Washington. While there, he and Charles' two older brothers worked as laborers on the family farm.

Charles Auer applied to the US Marine Corps on April 20, 1917, at Bakersfield, California, where he was living at the time. He was

---

[2] While researching for this book, I found a citation for a John F. Auer who received the Medal of Honor (MoH) while part of the Navy during the peacetime, on November 20, 1883. He was only one of 193 who received MoH during peacetime. While on duty, a young French boy fell overboard and John jumped in to save him, which he did. It does not appear that there is any relation between John F. and Charles as John was born and raised in New York, and after leaving the military he went back to New York, where he died in 1951.

[3] While the Stonehenge plaque has the date of birth as the correct month and day, the year, as per military documents, is 1893, not 1894.

approved and then officially enlisted on April 27, 1917, at Mare Island, California. He was stationed at Mare Island until June 20, 1917, when he was reassigned to Quantico, Virginia. Shortly after his reassignment to Quantico, he joined the 20th Co. 5th Battalion Marine Corps on June 26, 1917. Initially classified as a cook 1st class on July 1, 1917, he was reclassified during his promotion to a mechanic.

Throughout his time in the Marine Corps, his conduct was pretty consistent. While in the beginning he had some issues with military efficiency, only scoring a 3.5 out of 5, his obedience and sobriety were always a 5 out of 5. From his initial conduct when reassigned to his death in 1918, his conduct rose from an average of 4.5 to 4.7, showing an increase with military efficiency and staying obedient and sober. At every transfer and semi-annual review, he never had any offenses and was seen as a good Marine.

After spending almost two months in Virginia training, Auer and his unit embarked on the USS Henderson on August 5, 1917, from Philadelphia to Tompkinsville, New York, arriving on August 7, 1917. The ship then left that same day to arrive at St. Nazaire, France, on August 20, 1917. Upon arriving in France, the 20th company, 3rd Battalion, 5th Regiment was detached from Navy command and assigned to the US Army. In early January 1918, Auer's unit was assigned a zone of advance. From March 17, 1918, to May 5, 1918, Auer's unit participated in action against the enemy in Verdun. During the Verdun campaign, Pvt. Charles Auer was field promoted to corporal on May 1, 1918.

Following Verdun, the 20th Company moved to Chateau-Thierry on June 1, 1918. As it was near where active fighting was occurring, the unit fought in both the Chateau-Thierry area as well as the Bois de Belleau area. Auer's burial case file states that his unit was present and actively in combat during the battle on June 6, June 21, and June 26. It was the Marine's attack of Hill 142 on the morning of June 6 that Cpl. Charles Auer was killed by shell fire. By the end of the day, Hill 142 was controlled by the Marines but at a very high cost, with nine officers, and the majority of the 342 men who were part of the battalion being killed.

Due to the battle that Auer fell in, his remains were buried following the battle's end, but the location was not reported to the US Army Graves Registration Service (GRS) until August 7, nearly two months after his death. His unit had buried his remains in Cemetery 57, Grave 2-A. There was nothing to indicate what grave was Auer's other than the paperwork. On September 13, 1918, a GRS unit disinterred Auer's remains and reburied him in Cemetery 62, Grave 75, which was located 500 meters from Lucy-le-Bocage on Lucy-le-Bocage-Torcy road. GRS identified both the remains and the new grave with two metal identification tags.

On June 3, 1919, GRS removed his body from the small cemetery and reburied it at the National Cemetery at Belleau Woods, Aisne, Plot 1, Section G, Grave 15. At Belleau Woods, GRS used metal pipes to indicate grave plots, and small tinfoil plaques with the service member's name, and at times attached the small round identification tag. While there was no identification tag on the body, the tag was attached to the pipe, therefore further confirming the identity of the remains.

It was at Belleau Woods that Auer's remains stayed until his father requested that his remains be brought back to the United States and interred at Arlington National Cemetery. On July 16, 1921, GRS disinterred Auer's remains, checked against former records to ensure identification was accurate, and placed the remains in a casket for the return to the United States.

On August 27, 1921, Charles' remains, along with those of 86 other service members who died overseas, were transported from Hoboken, New Jersey, where they arrived from France to Rosslyn, Virginia. His remains were permanently interred at some point between August 30 and September 1 of that year at Arlington National Cemetery, Grave 18-2563. The dates are conflicting in official records, and that could partially be due to the number of remains being interred and when the official was finally able to fill out the necessary documents.

Following the war, Auer's father received a letter from a Lieutenant Colonel from the Adjutant & Inspector that listed the medals and other awards that Auer, or his unit, received during their tenure in combat. The letter that his father received included the following medals and other awards:

1 Victory Medal
1 Aisne Defense Battle Clasp

1 Defensive Battle Clasp
2 Silver Stars
2 Bronze Stars

Due to Auer's bravery on the field, he was cited for such, and recommended for the Distinguished Service Cross (DSC) by General Pershing, himself. However, he was also cited for a Navy Cross as he was a US Marine stationed with the Army. Research into lists for those individuals who received the DSC and the Navy Cross contradicted what the documentation states.[4] Although current research does not have Auer as a DSC recipient, both his father on July 20, 1922, and his mother, Rose Auer, on September 10, 1925, signed and dated a letter as having received the DSC. Officially, according to the US Marine Corps, Cpl. Auer was awarded the Navy Cross and not the DSC.

Documentation from Auer's burial case file does state that he received the Navy Cross and the lists currently available substantiate that. The citation that accompanied the DSC and the Navy Cross to his parents both read as follows:

"Charles Auer, Corporal, 20th Company, 5th Regiment, United States Marine Corps, killed in action at Chateau Thierry, France, June

---

[4] After speaking with USMC on November 27, 2018, the reason why it does not list Auer as a recipient is that even though he was awarded one by the US Army, because he was a Marine, he could not receive that medal, and therefore was officially awarded the Navy Cross. The medals were sent to his mother and father, but if he had survived, he would not have been able to wear the DSC on his uniform.

6, 1918. He gave the supreme proof of that extraordinary heroism which will serve as an example to hitherto untried troops."

Dewey V. Bromley

Dewey V. Bromley was born on July 13, 1898, the eighth of ten children, to Herrick and May Bromley of Yakima County, Washington.

He enlisted into the US Army and was assigned to Troop I, 15th Cavalry. On March 14, 1918, Pvt. Bromley shipped from Hoboken, New Jersey, to France aboard the SS Aeolus. Not long after he arrived in France, he became ill. Pvt. Bromley died on April 13, 1918, from broncho-pneumonia. Immediately following his death, he was buried at the post cemetery at Camp de Coetquidan on April 15, 1918, in Grave 23. One identification tag was buried with the remains, while the other was nailed to a stake at the foot of the grave.

At some point, one of two things happened: either GRS disinterred Pvt. Bromley and reinterred him in Grave 31, at the American cemetery at St. Malo-de-Beignon (Coetquidan) in the Morbihan region of France, or the remains they disinterred from Grave 31 were not Pvt. Bromley, even though records state "bottle record hospital checks with GRS records." Due to the fact that he initially was interred with an identification tag, along with a stake with an identification tag marking the grave, those should have still been present.[5] Pvt. Bromley was disinterred on December 1, 1921, in preparation for his final burial on September 13, 1922, in Grave 18, Block B, Row 33 at Oise-Aisne Cemetery, Seringes-et-Nesles in Aisne, France.

When GRS began to disinter remains, Pvt. Bromley's mother was asked if she wanted his remains returned to United States soil, in which she indicated that she did not. Furthermore, she indicated that if his remains were to be returned, that she wanted them in a national cemetery and not a local one.

Even though she was invited, Pvt. Bromley's mother did not travel as part of the Gold Star Mothers and Widows Pilgrimage in 1930, 1931, or 1932. In 1930, she indicated that she would rather them send her the money that they would have spent on her to travel. When they refused, she demanded to know why it mattered how the money was spent, because she needed the money more than a trip. The next year,

---

[5] The records I received from NPRC, among other places, may not be complete due to the fire at NPRC in 1972, and these are the only remaining records. Due to the number of burials and disinterments, it would be near impossible to determine if the grave they disinterred was Bromley's or if it was another.

she stated that she did not want to travel, but then a week later telegrammed the government to let them know that she was instead declining the invitation. When requested as to if she wanted to take part in the last year, 1933, she indicated that yes, she would like to see her son's grave.

While on the trip, Mrs. Bromley had numerous medical issues but was able to still participate in all the activities that the US Government had planned.

On June 7, 1933, Pvt. Bromley's mother traveled from Olympia, Washington, across the country to New York City via train. Once there, she and her daughter, Mrs. May Spregel, were transported via SS Washington as part of the Gold Star Mothers and Widows Pilgrimage. Due to the government setting specific rules regarding who could travel, Mrs. Spregel had to pay her own way, including arrangements for any day trips and sightseeing once in France.

Pvt. Bromley is permanently interred in the Oise-Aisne American Cemetery and Memorial in Fere-en-Tardenois, Departement de l'Aisne, Picardie, France.

John W. Cheshier

John Wilburn Cheshier was born June 13, 1890, in Ukiah, California, to John (J.M.) and Clara (Carter) Cheshier. His family lived in California until sometime between the 1900 census and the 1910 census. He registered for the draft on June 5, 1917, stating Lucas, Washington, as his place of residence. On December 8, 1917, he enlisted into the US Army at Vancouver Barracks, Washington.

He was assigned to the 6th Battalion, 20th Engineers, Forestry Department, out of Fort Vancouver, Washington. Cheshier was thought to be one of the first from Klickitat County's 300 soldiers and sailors to be sent to France.

On January 24, 1918, Pvt. Cheshier, along with at least twenty-three other soldiers from Company F, 6th Battalion, 20th Engineers, left New York, New York, on the SS Tuscania, a luxury liner that was used by the United States to send troops to Great Britain. On February 5, 1918, seven miles off the Mull of Oa, with more than 2,000 American soldiers on board, the German U-Boat UB-77 torpedoed and sank the Tuscania. Of those on board, 210 perished, including Pvt. Cheshier, either by drowning or by being thrown against the rocks by the North Channel currents.

The sinking of the USS Tuscania was an event that rocked the United States. Not only was it an act of war against a civilian liner, but also this was the first event that resulted in a large loss of life. The official bulletins from the time frequently referred to the USS Tuscania as the government attempted to ascertain how many service members were deceased or injured, and if dead, where the bodies were. Because of the delay in communication, it took months for the US government to finally account for all those on board.

Immediately after his death, he was interred in Kilnaughton, Fort Kilon, Islay Argyll, Scotland in Cemetery 154, Row 2, Grave 32. On March 1, 1920, Pvt. Cheshier's father requested that his son's remains remain in Scotland as Island Islay provided a good burial location. However, if his comrades wished for his remains to return to the US, then his remains should be interred at the National Cemetery, and to just let him know what the decision was. Also, if return was decided, that a date for final funeral be furnished. GRS had begun to disinter remains, and by the time the cablegram arrived from J.M. that requested permanent interment in Europe, it was too late. On July 26,

1920, GRS disinterred Pvt. Cheshier, who was interred with an ID tag, and by the time he was disinterred it had deteriorated by corrosion to only read "J.W. Hesie, Co F. Bn. 20 Engrs. 32." Since there was additional documentation, GRS concluded that this was the correct body.

On October 18, 1920, a representative from Dental Corps and a representative from Quartermaster Corps, along with multiple attendants, accompanied the remains of forty-nine soldiers from Hoboken, New Jersey, to Rosslyn, Virginia, for final burial at Arlington. On October 22, 1920, Pvt. John W. Cheshier was interred with full military honors in Arlington National Cemetery in Grave 18-1023.

Richard E. Childs

Richard Evan Childs was born July 15, 1893, in Britton, South Dakota, to Frank O. and Mary (Evans) Childs.[6] Richard Childs was part of the first class to graduate from White Salmon's Columbia High school, in 1912. After graduation, Childs bought his own farm near his parent's residence and lived and worked there.

When he registered for the draft on July 15, 1917, he listed White Salmon as his home, and farmer as his occupation. He enlisted in the US Army on October 3, 1917. Soon after, Cpl. Childs was assigned to B Co., 316th Engineers, 91st Division.

---

[6] Military records state his birthday is July 15, 1893. However, the obituary and another record state his birthday as July 14, 1893.

The unit was shipped from Camp Lewis, Washington, to France in July 1918. During the Battle of Argonne on September 29, 1918, Cpl. Childs was reported missing by his chain of command. Later that same day, he was officially reported killed in action. His remains were initially buried on the battlefield on October 11, 1918, at Foret d'Argonne, Exermont, Ardennes in an isolated Grave 1. Cpl. Childs was buried with his identification tag, and another tag was attached to the cross that marked his grave. On June 11, 1919, Cpl. Child's remains were disinterred from his isolated grave and reinterred on the same day in the Meuse-Argonne American Cemetery 1232, Grave 114, Section 103, Plot 3 in Romagne Meuse.

Following the first disinterment and reburial, the government began to receive letters from Cpl. Child's family. His brother, Pvt. John O. Childs, was also actively serving in France when news was delivered that Cpl. Childs had been injured and/or killed. Due to the discrepancy in information, both Pvt. John Childs, his sister, Carrie, an RN in Hood River, and their father all requested confirmation of status regarding Cpl. Childs.

Cpl. Childs' father requested that his son's remains be returned to the United States for burial. He was disinterred from Argonne American Cemetery on August 9, 1921, and the long process of returning home to White Salmon, Washington, began. Immediately following his disinterment, the remains were transferred from the cemetery to Antwerp, Belgium. On September 6, 1921, Cpl. Childs remains traveled from Antwerp to Hoboken, New Jersey, on the USAT Wheaton. Once there, military transport delivered the remains of Cpl. Childs, along with the remains of twenty-three other service members who had died in France, to Portland, Oregon, and the transport to their final destinations.

Cpl. Richard Childs is permanently interred in the West Klickitat District 01 Cemetery in White Salmon, Washington. Because of his sacrifice, the American Legion in White Salmon changed their name to the Evan Childs American Legion Post 87 prior to his funeral that occurred before October 7, 1921.[7]

---

[7] This was the earliest mention of the "Evan Childs American Legion post" which was found in White Salmon's *The Enterprise* October 7, 1921, page 7.

William O. Clary

William Osbin Clary was born on October 31, 1895, to Charles and Ida (Delap) Clary in Goldendale, Washington.[8] William was the third of four children born to his mother Ida before her death. The children were Eunice, the oldest and only daughter, and then John, William, and Manual. William's parents were originally from Missouri and the family moved to Washington at some point between 1889 and 1895.[9]

---

[8] There is a discrepancy on his birthdate. The military records state that his birthdate is October 31, 1895. However, the census records and the headstone at IOOF Mountain View show October 31, 1894. The only official documents state his birthdate is 1895.

[9] Many sources, including WikiTree, had previously connected a William F. Clary whose parents were Frank and Mary with William O. Clary whose parents were Charles and X. What is interesting is, during this period, Goldendale was not that large of a community, yet included two Clary families. Charles' family moved from Missouri, and Frank's family came from Canada. William F. was born June 4, 1894, while William O. was born October 31, 1895. It is no wonder that many resources

William signed his draft registration card on June 5, 1917, in Spring Creek precinct. At the time, he was a farmer, working for his father in Spring Creek, Washington. His exact enlistment date is unknown, partially due to the fact that his military records were likely part of the NPRC fire and partially because his enlistment and time in the military were slightly different than many who joined.

Due to his background, Pvt. Clary was sent to Vancouver Barracks to be part of a newly formed division. The Spruce Production Division was created to assist the war effort in providing wood for production of aircraft. In its prime, there were over 50,000 military personnel working in the Washington and Oregon forests and associated lumber mills. What is interesting about this division is that many of the soldiers selected for these positions never attended basic training, and were essentially exempt from being sent to France. They also took many men who were over the age of 40, but otherwise in good health.[10] Pvt. Clary was assigned to the 125th Squadron, which had the Eagle Gorge section of the Puget Sound region.

Pvt. William O. Clary died in the base hospital at Fort Lawton, Washington, on January 4, 1919, due to broncho-pneumonia. According to official documents, his death was in the line of duty. Furthermore, it was not a result of his own willful misconduct, which meant that his next of kin, his father, Charles, would receive full death benefits.

---

had the two families confused. Both men filled out their draft cards in the same location, but one was June 1917, and the other was September 1918.

[10] For more information about the Spruce Production Division, Robert Swanson created a very informative website located at http://swansongrp.com/spruce.html. A good book regarding this division is Rod Crossley's Soldiers in the Woods.

Clary's remains were shipped to his father who was at that time still living in Goldendale, Washington. His remains are interred at the IOOF Mountain View Cemetery in Goldendale, Washington, as W.O. Clary.

James D. Duncan

James Donald Duncan was born July 15, 1897, the second child, and oldest son of Edgar and Elizabeth (Coate) Duncan in Troy, Ohio. Prior to enlisting in the US Army, he lived in Trout Lake, Washington. As of his death, he was the only individual to have enlisted from Trout Lake.

He enlisted in the Army in late April 1917 in Camas, Washington, and was assigned as a recruit to the 17th Recruiting Company, Cavalry unassigned. James was residing in Fort McDowell, California, following his enlistment. On June 16, 1917, he died of acute nephritis due to measles.

Recruit Duncan's uncle, D.W. Coate, an agent for the Shriners in San Francisco, found out that his nephew's remains were not immediately cared for and began a letter campaign on June 19, 1917. In the first letter, he stated that if it were not for him, he believes that the remains would have languished even longer, and that it was due to the fact that Duncan was only a recruit and not yet a service member. He goes on to state that the family had been part of the military or worked for the government since the Civil War and that it was not for "such negligence as this, and act that is beyond being excused for." He even states that remains on the battlefields of Europe would not have been left in such a manner, as the Red Cross would not allow it.

From communication between the military and D.W. Coate, it appears that Duncan passed away early on a Saturday and his remains were delivered to a local embalmer, a Mr. Reilly. The military immediately notified Rct. Duncan's mother via telegram, but by the time that Elizabeth Duncan replied stating that she would like the remains returned home, it was later in the afternoon and the Quartermaster depot who was assigned the task of transporting remains was closed on Sundays, and so it was not until Monday that documents were transmitted between military offices. Due to the need for invoices and such, remains were not shipped until Tuesday morning.

What is interesting is that upon that communication, D.W. Coate requested additional information on July 2, 1917, regarding Duncan's enlistment date, date of sickness onset, and did he "first have measles and did nephritis develop from measles, or did he have either one?" He states that his sister, Duncan's mother, requested this information. The only reply that he received was notification from A.D.

Kremmers, a Captain with the Medical Corps. In the reply, it stated that "Under paragraph 824 Army Regulations this information cannot be furnished. If desired, request can be made through the Adjutant General of the Army."

Other than communication among themselves, it does not appear that Mr. D.W. Coate requested any additional information after being told that they could not provide that information. It wasn't until 1919 that Duncan's father wrote to his senator, Wesley Jones of Washington, as to how he could procure a headstone for Duncan's grave.

Rct. James Duncan is permanently interred in the Trout Lake Cemetery in Trout Lake, Washington.

Harry Gotfredson

Harry Gotfredson was born April 4, 1894, in Bickleton, Washington, to Rasmus and Lottie (Hull) Gotfredson. He was the third of five living children to the couple. When Harry registered for the draft on June 5, 1917, in Alder Creek precinct, he was living on a farm near Bickleton and working as a farmer.[11] He formally enlisted in the Army in October 1917 at Camp Lewis in Washington.

He was soon transferred to Camp Mills and then to France. After his first tour in France, he was sent to Winchester, England, and served with the Military Police before returning to France in June 1918. He was part of the M.G. Company, 165th Infantry, 42nd Division.

---

[11] While the plaque at Stonehenge states that his date of birth was May 6, 1894, Army enlistment records record his birthdate as April 4, 1894.

Originally, Pvt. Gotfredson was listed as killed in action on July 30, 1918. However, following an investigation into his death and subsequent burial, it was determined by a Captain who was involved, that Pvt. Gotfredson was found dead on July 29, 1918, during one of the initial sweeps. According to the Captain, he took part in a battle for the Bois-de-Colas and the Meurcy Farm, which was just beyond the River Ourcq, northeast of Villers-sur-Fere. When the battle was over and the French and Americans had captured the area, Pvt. Gotfredson's remains were found. He was buried where he laid as per guidelines at the time.

The Chaplain of his unit stated in the official grave location document that Pvt. Gotfredson's remains were interred right outside the south wall of a cemetery at Villers-sur-Fere, Aisne, with no identification tag or other identifying marker. This includes no marker, no cross, no bottle, or any other form of identification. On September 18, a Grave Location Blank was filled out again, stating that the burial did not have any grave marker. However, soon after that on September 28, another Grave Location Blank was filled out, stating his burial was at Cemetery 1 at Villers-sur-Fere, Grave 26, and that a nameplate and cross were used to mark the burial.

On May 31, 1919, the GRS disinterred Pvt. Gotfredson from Cemetery 1, Grave 26, Map 33 S.E. Com Villers-sur-Fere, Aisne. He was disinterred with no identification and the first form dated June 3, 1919, stated that Pvt. Gotfredson was in a trench with thirty-three other remains. This would make sense due to the number of soldiers killed in action, and the expedited nature of needing to bury the remains. However, a "corrected" copy dated June 25, 1919, and signed by the same individual stated that Pvt. Gotfredson was buried five feet deep, with no identification, however, there was a grave marker with his information on it. That same day, Pvt. Gotfredson was reinterred in Cemetery 608 Seringes-et-Nesles, Aisne, Grave 102, Plot 2, Section L.

In 1921, the US government was ready to begin returning remains to the United States at the request of families. Pvt. Gotfredson's mother had passed away, and so his next of kin was his brother, Albert. On January 25, 1921, Pvt. Gotfredson's remains were still located at Grave 102, Plot 2, Section L, when a compilation of remains was created in anticipation of his next of kin's request for return of remains. In February 1921, Albert requested that his brother's remains remain in one of the many American cemeteries in France.

On May 6, 1921, knowing that the next of kin did not want the remains returned, they disinterred the remains in order to maintain some form of precision in the cemetery. This was not an uncommon practice, especially when GRS believed that a wartime cemetery may become a more permanent resting place. GRS reburied him on the same day, in the same cemetery, Grave 200, Plot 4, Section L. At this time, two skulls and two jaws were found in the grave. Unable to determine which skull accompanied the body, they seemingly made the determination and stated, "...of head buried with body." Also included was a letter addressed to Harry Gotfied---, a notebook with "Gotfredson," and two corroded identification tags that were buried with the remains.

On January 8, 1926, a report was made that stated Pvt. Gotfredson's remains were interred in Cemetery 608, Grave 26, scratched out and changed to 46, Row 1, Block B. The cemetery has the same code as it did before, so GRS may have changed its naming practices from when Pvt. Gotfredson was interred in 1921 and this report in 1926. On January 25, 1927, another compilation of remains was created which stated that his next of kin did not want remains returned, as well as the location of burial, and his burial location as Grave 102, Plot 2, Section L.

Cemetery 608 would become the permanent cemetery of Oise-Aisne near the town of Seringes-et-Nesles. In anticipation of an influx of remains, GRS created new plots and moved remains around in order to present a more functioning and visually appealing location. On February 25, 1928, Pvt. Gotfredson's remains were disinterred from Grave 46, Block B, Row 1, in which two skulls were located, as well as two USNG collar ornaments and one MG X C collar ornament.[12] His remains were reinterred that same day in Grave 22, Block B, Row 1. Documents created in 1929 and 1937 both stated the burial location as Grave 22, Block B, Row 1. From all records available, it would appear both skulls were buried in Grave 22, Block B, Row 1.

Pvt. Gotfredson's remains are still interred at the Oise-Aisne American Cemetery and Memorial in Picardie, France.[13]

---

[12] X in a collar ornament denotes crossed rifles versus an actual X.
[13] His remains as per the ABMC website are Grave 22, Plot B, Row 1 with a date of death of July 29, 1918.

Robert F. Graham

Robert Floyd Graham was born on February 29, 1896, in Clifton County, Kansas, to Thomas and Flora (Felt) Graham. He enlisted in the Oregon Coast Artillery on March 25, 1917. He was assigned to the 8th Co. Oregon Coast Artillery, part of the Oregon Guard. Prior to his death, he had been assigned as a clerk in the Quartermaster's office.[14]

Pvt. Graham contracted cerebrospinal meningitis and died at St. Vincent's Hospital in Portland, Oregon, on April 17, 1917.[15]

---

[14] There is not a lot of information regarding the Oregon Coast Artillery's service overseas.

[15] Pvt. Graham's brother had contracted cerebrospinal meningitis and had passed away just a few months before him. Due to the disease and his relative sickness period, his mother and younger brother had to be quarantined following his death to ensure they did not contract it from him prior to his enlistment.

Pvt. Graham is permanently interred next to his brother Willard at Gray Butte Cemetery, Culver, Oregon.

Thomas E. Hovey

Thomas Edward Hovey was born in White Salmon, Washington, to Peter Hovey and his wife.[16]

After enlisting in Washington for the Army, Pvt. Hovey was assigned to F Co. 344th Infantry Regiment, 88th Division. On June 11, 1918, Pvt. Hovey and his unit were transported from Hoboken, New Jersey, to France aboard the United States Army Transport (USAT) Northumberland.

---

[16] Thomas' mother passed away before he did and there is not confirmation regarding his mother's name. I found information concerning his father having married a woman named "Lena Frelander." Every census prior to 1920 did not have Peter married or with children. The 1920 census shows that he was a widow living by himself. All that is known is that Thomas' mother and father were both from Norway.

In October 1918, Pvt. Hovey fell sick and was sent to a hospital in Toul, France. Unable to become well again, Pvt. Hovey died October 31, 1918, from bronchopneumonia. He was buried at the Cemetery of Justice, Hospital Group, Toul, Meurthe-et-Moselle in France in Grave 728.

His father, living in Minnesota at the time of Pvt. Hovey's death, requested that his son's remains be returned to the United States. Pvt. Hovey's remains were shipped from the cemetery in Toul on February 13, 1922, to Antwerp, and left Antwerp for Hoboken, New Jersey, on March 3, 1922, aboard the USAT Cambria. On April 14, 1922, Pvt. Hovey's remains were shipped from Brooklyn, New York, to his father's residence in Long Prairie, Minnesota.

Louis Leidl

Louis Leidl was born on March 5, 1894, in Goldendale, Washington, to Wendelin and Lissette (Koehler) Leidl. After graduating from Goldendale High School in 1912, Louis attended Washington State College and was part of the Washington Alpha chapter of the Sigma Phi Epsilon fraternity.

On June 5, 1917, Louis registered for the draft. He listed his occupation as farmer, but also listed that he had two years of service as a corporal in the Washington State Guard. Leidl enlisted into the United States Army on August 31, 1917, in Seattle, Washington. For a short time, he was a private with F Co. 10th Engineers. Quickly, he was transferred to D Co., 501st Engineers Service Battalion, 7th Engineer Regiment, 5th Division, and promoted to second lieutenant.

The 501st Engineers Service Battalion, along with 2nd Lt. Leidl, sailed on November 26, 1917, from Hoboken, New Jersey, to France on the SS Aeolus. As part of the engineer regiment, the 7th saw combat in numerous locations over the following year. On October 14, 1918, Leidl's unit was actively engaged against the enemy near Cunel, France. He was last seen by his commanding officer fighting alongside his men while they attempted to recapture the two towns of Cunel and Romagne. He went over a hill with another soldier. That soldier was killed and buried; however, Leidl's fate was undetermined. Some days later, an unidentified set of remains belonging to a second lieutenant were located near the area that Leidl had gone missing.

Second Lt. Leidl was initially listed as missing in action, and his family was updated on that status. The military investigated his death and subsequent burial. One of the ways they did this was to speak with individuals who were present during the attack, death, or burial to determine the location and any pertinent facts. During the investigation, Thomas Roan wrote a letter that stated:

> 1st Lt. Leidl was killed the morning of Oct. 14 during the Meuse Argonne drive. Id did not see it happen. They buried him up there. I made the cross for his grave. It was about 3 ½ ft. high and 3 ft wide, marked with his name, number, rank, regiment, company, the time he was killed, and a diamond for the fifth division. The graves are at Cunelle near the Madelon Farm. They took photographs of them all.[17]

---

[17] Letter from a Thomas Roan, attached to Burial Case File for 2nd Lt. Louis Leidl.

On May 12, 1919, 2nd Lt. Leidl's remains were disinterred from Grave 20, B.A. Cemetery in Cunel, Meuse, France, and reinterred that same day in Grave 141, Section 89, Plot 3, Argonne American Cemetery, Romagne, Meuse, France. There was no identification on the remains or on the grave marker. The body had a 5th Division Engineers insignia along with an officer cap with insignia and an officer braid on the sleeve of the blouse. When he was interred, the grave marker was inscribed with "Unknown US Soldier U-3572."

On August 17, 1921, 2nd Lt. Leidl was disinterred from Grave 141, Section 89, Plot 3. After being sent to the morgue, he was reinterred on November 18, 1921, in the same cemetery, in Grave 32, Row 13, Block C. Again, there was no identification with the remains, other than one engineer insignia. Again, the remains were identified as "Unknown US Soldier, U-3572." It was not until December 28, 1922, that GRS connected Unknown US Soldier, U-3572 to that of 2nd Lt. Louis Leidl. For that reason, it was not until March 9, 1923, that the Leidl family received confirmation that 2nd Lt. Leidl's remains had been located and properly interred.

In 1930, his mother, Lissette Leidl, accepted the government's offer to travel to France to see her son's grave. Prior to travel, she requested that she be cabined with Mrs. Frances Willard, also from Washington, and that they be part of the same group while in France. Her wishes were granted, and her railroad ticket was adjusted as such. She traveled from Goldendale, Washington, on May 15, 1930, to New York City via railroad and then continued aboard the SS George Washington. While there, she experienced medical issues that resulted in her having to be hospitalized for three days before being discharged and allowed to continue with the trip.

    Lissette and two other mothers or widows decided that while they were in France, they would not immediately return home, and so their return transportation was canceled as per government guidelines. Lissette traveled to Germany, her home country, and stayed with her sibling and niece for thirteen days before returning to France. Two weeks after she was scheduled to return home, she sailed on the SS Harding from France at her own expense.

    As per government guidelines, mothers and widows were to write the War Department thanking them for the trip and letting them know how it went. Lissette wrote the War Department, as well as the local paper. On August 8, 1930, Lissette's letter regarding her trip was published in the *Klickitat County Agriculturist*, detailing her trip.[18]

    The American Legion post in Goldendale, Washington, changed its name to the "Louis Leidl American Legion post 116." Prior to his death, he had been a member of Post 116, and so following notification of his death, the name was changed to honor his sacrifice. This change occurred prior to March 22, 1923.

    Second Lt. Leidl is permanently interred at the Meuse-Argonne American Cemetery in Romagne, France.

---

[18] Copy of letter is available online due to length and size.

Carl A. Lester

Carl Lester was born October 6, 1888, in Purple Cane, Nebraska, to Clarence A. and Jennie (Avery) Lester. He was the third of eight siblings; however, Clarence listed his wife as having nine births on the 1900 census, meaning at some point one child died.

On June 5, 1917, Lester registered for the draft in Spring Creek, Klickitat County, Washington. He listed Centerville, Washington, as his home. At the time, he was a twenty-seven-year-old, single farmer working for himself.

Pvt. Lester was assigned to the 2nd Casual Co. Aviation Section, Signal Corps, stationed at Vancouver Barracks, Washington. While there, he contracted pneumonia and died on March 15, 1918. His remains were shipped to his father in Goldendale, Washington, on March 16, 1918.

Pvt. Lester is permanently interred at the IOOF Mountain View Cemetery in Goldendale, Washington.

Edward J. Lindblad

Edward James Lindblad was born on March 25, 1899, in Anaconda, Montana, to Erick and Anna Lindblad. He applied to the Marine Corps on April 26, 1917, in North Yakima, Washington. During that time, he was living in Six Prong, Washington. Approval was not immediate as Edward was underweight, according to Marine Corps standards, so the Major General Commandant had to grant a waiver for him to formally enlist. After being approved, he formally enlisted in the Marine Corps on May 3, 1917, at Mare Island, California. Initially, Pvt. Lindblad was not a great Marine; in fact, his military efficiency score was only a 3.5 while he was stationed at Mare Island.

Pvt. Lindblad was stationed in Quantico, Virginia, from July 14, 1917, until he embarked on the SS Henderson on January 19, 1918. By this point, his overall military efficiency score had gone up to between a

4 and 4.5. On February 8, 1918, Lindblad, along with the 6th Marines who were attached to the US Army, began serving. On June 2, he was injured in action, and he was evacuated to SOS hospital on June 10, 1918. He was then assigned to a Replacement Battalion from June 24 through September 10, when he rejoined the 79th Co.

While assigned to the 79th Co. 6th Marines, he was initially marked as missing in action on September 15, 1918. However, when he did not show back up for muster on September 25, 1918, his unit and the Marine Corps dropped him from the muster rolls. His family received notification in October that Pvt. Lindblad had gone missing, but there was no further information. It was not until his body was recovered in early November 1918 that they sent correspondence to his mother and father that, in fact, Pvt. Lindblad had been killed during the initial battle and had not truly been missing. It is believed by the Marine Corps that he died on or immediately following September 15, 1918. Although it took about two months, on November 19, 1918, Pvt. Lindblad was buried west of the road near Charey. On June 12, 1919, Pvt. Lindblad was disinterred from an isolated grave at Charey, Meurthe-et-Moselle and interred the same day in Grave 31, Section 18, Plot 1 at St. Mihiel American Cemetery.

He was disinterred on July 13, 1922, from Grave 31, Section 18, Plot 1 of St. Mihiel Cemetery to be reinterred the same day in Grave 23, Block C, Row 4. On his remains there was only a Catholic medal with no other forms of identification. On the grave marker, there was identification stating Pvt. Lindblad had been buried in that location. GRS stated that there was nothing to disprove identification, either.

Following Pvt. Lindblad's death, he was awarded the Victory medal with ribbon, Aisne Battle Clasp, St. Mihiel Battle Clasp, Defensive Sector Clasp, and three bronze stars. His mother, being his next of kin, received these medals along with notification of awards on December 20, 1920.

Pvt. Lindblad's mother, Anna, took part in the 1930 Gold Star Mothers and Widows Pilgrimage. She traveled from Bellingham, Washington, to New York City via railroad. Once there, she traveled to France on the SS President Roosevelt. She returned home on the SS America and then via railroad.

Pvt. Lindblad is permanently interred in Grave 23, Row 4, Plot C at St. Mihiel American Cemetery in Thiaucourt, Meurthe-et-Moselle, France.

Henry O. Piendl

Born September 16, 1893, to Jacob and Emily (McCarty) Piendl, Henry O. Piendl and his family were at the time living in Alder Creek, Washington. He was the third of five children; his older siblings, brother Mark and sister Belle, and younger siblings, sister Velma and brother John, rounded out the family. His father was from Germany and arrived into the United States in 1853. Emily, his mother, was an Iowan, born in 1858. In 1910, the family was living in Alder Creek, Washington, and Henry's parents had been married for thirty years.

Pvt. Piendl was inducted into the United States Army on October 4, 1917, in Yakima, Washington.

While stationed with Company I, 9th Infantry, 2nd Division, on July 30, 1918, Pvt. Piendl and his unit came under fire. They were either attached to or working alongside French units in the Chaudun (Aisne) region of France. Piendl, along with multiple American and French soldiers, was killed. In this instance, it was French soldiers who initially buried the dead, not just the French who fell, but also Americans.

Later that year, a nametag of Piendl's was located by the GRS and a request to the Company Commander of Company I, 9th Infantry, was made as to the circumstances regarding Pvt. Piendl. Obviously by this point, his company knew that he had been killed, so a report transmitted back relayed that information.

On May 24, 1928, GRS received a letter from the French that listed twenty separate entries for individuals who died and were buried on July 30, 1918. Pvt. Piendl was listed, but did not have a grave number, only that it was a "Field south of Chaudun." Further investigation occurred with a letter being sent to Piendl's mother, asking about the state of his teeth. This was in hopes of possibly identifying one of the unknowns that was interred in the same location as Piendl. The list the French delivered with twenty entries had ten named soldiers, six unknown American soldiers, and four unknown German soldiers. The French named Piendl in the document, but when GRS disinterred the remains, the remains did not match the names. Furthermore, a separate investigation was begun regarding two of the named graves, including one with a grave number attached, and at least two unknowns, U-827 and U-334.

On November 10, 1930, the French military sent another form to GRS that incorporated numerous transmissions of burials into one. Titled "Translation of French Report of Burials of American Soldiers Killed in Soissons Sector Sent Under Cover of Letter of November 10, 1930, From Europe." In this document, under "Death Reported July 30, 1918 – Form No. 8 Made Out July 30, 1918 by 300th R.I.T.," Line 183 is Henry I. Piendl with the rank of private, no effects, and a burial that just states, "South of Chaudun."[19]

After the congressional mandate to allow widows and mothers to travel to Europe, the US War Department mailed Emily, Henry's mother, a letter on June 25, 1930, and it included her statement that Henry was not married, and that he was survived by a mother, herself. On August 12, 1930, they requested information on if she would like to make the pilgrimage in which she stated that she was not interested in attending the 1931 pilgrimage. To confirm Henry's marital status, another letter on March 12, 1931, was sent to his mother, to which Emily responded that he was not married.

On June 15, 1931, the War Department again scheduled a place for Emily to travel to Europe and she replied with "I could not stand the Trip." Not to be deterred, the War Department replied with a letter on August 11, 1931, indicating that competent personnel will be provided to care for the mothers and widows. Any medical necessities will be arranged along with medical personnel. They further said that many

---

[19] The report sent November 1930 had Piendl's middle name as 'I' when it is actually Orrin. Since there were no effects on the body, it is assumed that a document handwritten with the O looking like an I was used when making the official list. That, or they used other soldier's recollections on what the dead's middle names were. Upon further research, no other "H. Piendl" died during World War I.

mothers of advanced age and poor health traveled and were better for it. Emily replied with a letter that stated:

"Thank you for the invitation, I can not plan on taking a trip my health is poor. I feel that I will never see 1933. If I understand rite(sic) Henry Orrin Piendl's grave was never found. I shall never forget my poor boy every time I get those letters from the war department. It worries me and I fear sad. I am a widow living with my son."

In the last round of pilgrimages, the War Department invited Emily Piendl again in 1932. Sadly, the response to the US War Department's 1932 request was from Belle Piendl, Henry' sister. In her response, she informed them that her mother passed away May 12, 1932, just two months before the letter was mailed.

To this day, Pvt. Henry Orrin Piendl is still on the rolls for World War I missing in action. His remains may be interred as an "unknown" in one of ABMC's French cemeteries. Or he may still be in the field south of Chaudun where he was originally interred by the French on July 30, 1918. Unless found, his name will forever be immortalized on the Tablets of the Missing at the Aisne-Marne American Cemetery in Belleau, France.

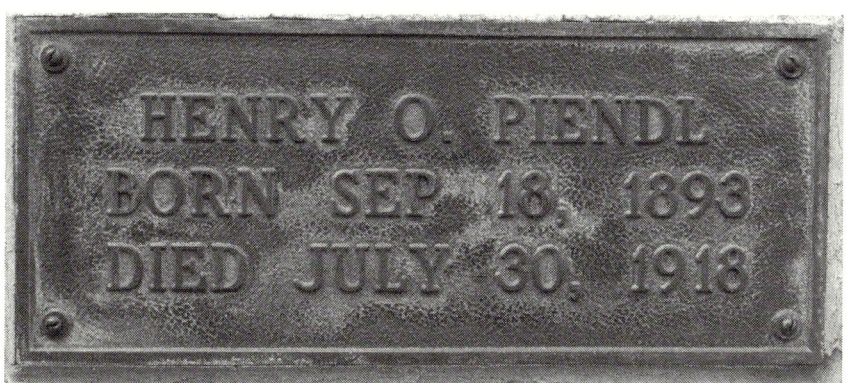

Robert F. Venable

Robert Francis Venable was born on September 29, 1898, in Goldendale, Washington, to Andrew Venable and Laura (Wing) Venable.[20]

He enlisted in the US Navy on April 10, 1917, in Portland, Oregon. Immediately following his enlistment, Venable attended NTS San Francisco where he graduated on April 22, 1917. Immediately following that, he was assigned to the USS San Diego from April 23 until May 7 when he became ill. As a seaman 2nd class, he was stationed at Mare Island, California.

---

[20] Prior to Robert's enlistment, his mother had remarried and changed her name to Troutman and moved to Michigan and then Indiana. Gladys, Robert's younger sister, remained with her mother.

On May 7, 1917, he was transferred to the Naval Hospital at Mare Island, California, with a diagnosis of broncho-pneumonia. Sea. 2nd class Venable died on May 21, 1917. While his mother did not reside in Goldendale when he died, she had a brother who still did. His remains were transported to his uncle, Willard Wing, in Goldendale, Washington.

Sea. 2nd class Venable is permanently interred at the IOOF Mountain View Cemetery in Goldendale, Washington.

Conclusion

If you notice, there was one individual who did not have a plaque. Thomas Hovey, from White Salmon, gave his all but for an unknown reason his name was not immortalized on Stonehenge. There are also small errors on dates of birth and death.

For those who did not look further than the stones, they may automatically assume that all fourteen men died in France during the war. However, this is not the case. This does not diminish the sacrifice the men and their families made for their country. The men still left their homes, and they still died an early death in the pursuit of service to their country. Just because they did not die to an enemy blow, does not mean they should not be remembered for being willing to risk it all.

This book has been a labor of love, and frustration. Frustration in that it took so long to get the records I needed. Frustration that not all the records still existed. But love in that I was able to show a bit of their story, their life beyond the stones.

Selected Bibliography

Instead of listing each individual and their respective Official Military Personnel File and Burial Case File, I instead list the record name and group. All of the official records are publicly available. This is by no means a complete list of the documents and newspaper articles that I have consulted. As previously stated, the fire that ravished NPRC took with it the majority of the Army military files.

Correspondence, Reports, Telegrams, Applications, and other Papers related to Burials of Service Personnel. Records of the Quartermaster General's Office, 1915-1939; Record Group 92; National Archives at St. Louis.

"Memorial to the Dead of World War I," Wagenweb.com http://wagenweb.org/klickitat/cem/stonehenge/index.html : 2018

Official Military Personnel Record. Records of the U.S. Department of the Army, National Archives at St. Louis.

Records of the Adjutant General's Office, 1905 – 1918, Record Group 407; National Archives, Washington, D.C.

Records of the Bureau of Naval Personnel, Record Group 024; National Archives at St. Louis.

Tuhy, John E. (1963), *Sam Hill: The Prince of Castle Nowhere,* Portland, Oregon: Timber Press.

"World War II Draft Registration Cards, 1917-1918." Database and images. Fold3.com. www.fold3.com : 2018

Appendix

All articles included in the appendix as well as articles that were deemed too large to fit are also available online at menbeyondthestones.com

Newspaper Articles from service members back home

THE ALLYN BOYS WRITE TO GOLDENDALE FRIENDS.

Camp Hancock
Augusta, Georgia

To the Editor:—

I received the "Sentinel" the other day and have read it from front to back.

I am to change my address soon but will let you know my new address as I like to get the "Sentinel" very much.

When leaving Goldendale to enlist I promised to write to all my friends, but, I find it a hard thing to do to so many, so will write you all at once through the columns of the Goldendale Sentinel.

I enlisted in the Aviation Section, Signal Corps, at Portland, Oregon, on December 5th, was taken to Vancouver barracks the same afternoon.

I stayed at Vancouver until Dec. 15th, when we were sent to Kelly Field at South San Antonio, Texas. We arrived there the night of Dec. 19th. We marched all over the camp looking for a place to sleep and at about 12 o'clock was put in a tent with my brother Valdie, and six fellows from New York.

There are soldiers at Kelly Field from every state in the union.

I always had an idea what the "Sunny South" was like but—Nix for mine! The land was just dust and the wind was fierce, sand storms a common occurance. Certainly nothing like the place where the "Sunshine and rain both meet."

There is a flying school at Kelly Field and during the day there are from five to fifty aeroplanes in the air at all times. But we soon get used to seeing them.

Have been here ever since, but have been transfered from one company to another several times. I am now in the 5th Company of the 2nd Motor Mechanics Reg. S. C. and do not think I will be transferred again soon. The 2nd M. M. Reg. has a volunteer Band and Valdie, my brother and I are playing with them.

Georgia is about like the Klickitat country. There is some pine timber here but all rather small. They raise a good deal of cotton and some water melons. We had about 2 inches of snow but it is just like summer now.

We expect to leave here soon. Don't know what date or where we will go. I think we will go across the pond in the near future.

Would be glad to hear from any or all of you. You see a letter to one of the boys in the Army is just like a stick of candy to a baby.

It is about time for retreat and I have to play in the band so will ring off for this time.

James H. Allyn, 5th Company 2nd M. M. Reg. S. C. A. E. F.

The Goldendale Sentinel (Goldendale, Wa.) March 7, 1918

Newspaper Articles regarding service members

JOHN CHESHIER AMONG LOST.

Today's paper give out the list of the lost on the transport Tuscania, among whom is the name of John Wilburn Cheshier. This will doubtless dispell any other hope of him being a survivor, as the list is from the government report. His death brings the war home to us, in Klickitat very forcibly. The deep sympathy of the community is extended the sorrowing family.

The Goldendale Sentinel (Goldendale, Wa.) February 14, 1918

OREGON GUARDSMAN DIES

Robert Graham's Father Comes From Goldendale for Body.

Robert Graham, 27 years old, who died at St. Vincent's Hospital on Tuesday evening, was a member of the Eighth Company of Oregon Coast Artillery, having joined the colors two weeks ago.

Several days ago Private Graham, who was assigned to duty with a recruiting officer in this city was taken ill with cerebro-spinal meningitis and was removed to the hospital and grew rapidly worse. His brother succumbed to the same malady a few months ago.

The young man's father, T. A. Graham, arrived in Portland from the family home at Goldendale, Wash., yesterday, and will supervise arrangements for the funeral, which probably will be held in Central Oregon.

Morning Oregonian (Portland, Or.) April 19, 1917

LEWIS LEIDL LISTED AS MISSING IN ACTION

The following wire has been received by W. Leidl and family, of Glenwood, which speaks for itself:

"We regret to inform you that Lt. Lewis Leidl is officially reported missing in action, Oct. 14. Further information when we receive it.— Harris, Adj. Gen."

Recent letters from him told of going into action the latter part of September and the first part of October. He had been recommended for bravery in action, and doubtless "carried on" in the thick of the fight. More definite word is hoped for daily. Red tape and the poor filing system is said to be responsible for the delay in receiving casualty lists from Washington, and many mistakes have occurred. By being listed in the "Missing in Action" column does not give great cause to worry, at least for the present. Daily mistakes are being corrected in the lists, and the reports are way behind. It is confidently expected that word will be received soon of a more definite nature.

The Goldendale Sentinel (Goldendale, Wa.) December 19, 1918

Edward J. Lindblad, Six Prong, Wash., is missing.

Morning Oregionian (Portland, Or.) November 8, 1918

GRIM REAPER CALLS IN THE COMMUNITY

CARL AVERY LESTER.

The funeral service of Private Carl Avery Lester was conducted at the Chapman Chapel on Tuesday afternoon. Rev. Henry T. Greene delivered the funeral address.

Private Lester was a younw man in 1888 and came to Klickitat in 1903, and has since lived here. He went into the Service last September and was a member of the Casusal Detachment Aviation Corps, stationed at Vancouver, Washington. He died on March 15th, aged 29 years.

He leaves to mourn his loss a father and mother; Mr. and Mrs. C. A. Lester, of Horseshoe Bend; six brothers—Marion S. of The Dalles; Herbert, of Wasco, Oregon; Henry George, Dudley and Bennie, who live with the parents. Two sisters survive him: Mrs. Gertrude Hoffman, of Fallbridge, and Ruth, who lives with the family at the Bend.

Private Lester was a young man of excellent qualities and was honored and respected by all who knew him. In the funeral address Rev. Greene paid a tribute to Private Lester and all others like him, who are defending the "flag and the Republic for which it stands." He drew a parallel between the life and work of a soldier in the service and that of all men, saying that when the order was given for "over the top," the soldier followed his leader, went with a purpose and with a passion.

The Goldendale Sentinel (Goldendale, Wa.) March 21, 1918

About the Author

Andretta holds a dual bachelors in history and sociology from Pacific University and a Master's degree in Diplomatic and Military Studies from Hawaii Pacific University. While working towards her Master's degree, Ms. Schellinger worked at the Joint POW/MIA Accounting Command which assisted in her love of the military and culture. She owns her own writing and research business Schellinger Research.

Made in the USA
Columbia, SC
04 April 2019